THE MENIERE EFFECT
HOW TO MANAGE THE LIFE CHANGING EFFECTS OF MENIERE'S

PAGE ADDIE PRESS
UNITED KINGDOM. AUSTRALIA

MENIERE MAN
AND THE BUTTERFLY

THE MENIERE EFFECT
HOW TO MANAGE THE LIFE CHANGING EFFECTS OF MENIERE'S

Copyright©2012 by Meniere Man

All rights reserved. No reproduction, copy or transmission of this Publication may be made without written permission from the author. No paragraph of this publication may be reproduced, copied or transmitted. Save with written permission or in accordance with provisions of the Copyright, Designs and Patents Act 1988, or under the terms of any license permitting limited copying, issued by the Copyright Licensing Agency, The Author has asserted his right to be identified as the author of this work in accordance with the Copyright, Design and Patents Act 1988

The Meniere Effect. How to Minimize the Meniere Effect on Family, Money, Lifestyle, Dreams and You. Meniere Man and the Butterfly. ISBN 978-0-9807155-4-5 is published by Page Addie, Australia, Page Addie, Australia is an imprint of Page-Addie Press, Great Britain. BIC Subject category: VFJB A catalogue record for this book is available from Australian National Library. 1. vertigo 2. dizziness. 3. dizzy. 4. Meniere's disease. 5 meniere 6. inner ear. 7. disease symptoms. 8 vestibular problems. 9. vertigo symptoms. 10 causes of vertigo. 11. imbalance in ear. 12. what is vertigo. 13 low salt. 14 coping with vertigo.

Disclaimer: The opinions in this book are strictly the Author's and in no way are meant to take the place of advice by medical professionals. This book is merely written to assist with information as experienced by the Author

THE
MENIERE
EFFECT

Contents

THE MENIERE EFFECT	9
THE DIAGNOSTIC EFFECT	15
THE FIRST EFFECTS OF MENIERE'S	21
THE BLACK HOLE EFFECT	31
THE EFFECT OF INFORMATION	35
THE MENIERE EFFECT ON YOUR JOB	63
THE NO EFFECT	89
THE EFFECT OF PLANNING	91
AN EFFECTIVE WAY OF MOVING ON	93
THE DIARY EFFECT	96
THE STRESS EFFECT	97
THE MENIERE EFFECT ON YOU	101
THE SABOTEUR EFFECT	103
THE RELAXATION EFFECT	105
TWENTY EFFECTIVE WAYS TO MANAGE MENIERE'S	108
EFFECTIVE MENIERE'S SUPPORT NETWORKS AND SOCIETIES	118
ABOUT MENIERE MAN	120
ADDITIONAL INFORMATION	123
MENIERE MAN BOOKS	124

THE MENIERE EFFECT

The term "butterfly effect" is based in chaos theory. The phrase refers to the idea that a butterfly's wings create tiny changes in the atmosphere that may ultimately change the weather. The flutter of tiny wings could create heavy rains in Florida, a flood in Florence, a tropical cyclone in Fiji or a tornado in Fargo.

The idea that one small butterfly could eventually have a far-reaching ripple effect on subsequent events first appeared in 1952 in *A Sound of Thunder,* a famous short story written by Ray Bradbury.

The idea that Meniere's disease could eventually have a far-reaching effect on love, life-style, family, friends, work and money, first appears in this book, *Meniere Man and the Butterfly*. This phenomenon of change is what I call the Meniere Effect.

The Meniere Effect is simple. You have a cause (Meniere's disease) and you have the effect (how this disease can affect aspects of your life). Just like the first "sound of thunder" from increased tinnitus makes you rush off to see your doctor. You undergo a series of tests with an ENT specialist. The results of audiology tests prove beyond a doubt that you have Meniere's disease.

You walk out of the surgery, diagnosed with a disease you have never heard of before. Meniere's disease. And while you focus on the physical act of coping with such awful news, the "wings of the butterfly" start flapping. The initial diagnosis causes a chain of events leading to unexpected changes in your life.

You don't wake up suddenly to financial and social chaos. But the ripple on effect of Meniere's disease will definitely continue on into your life. It's the cause and effect of having any long term condition or disease.

Nothing happens in isolation. The effects of Meniere's disease on your life happen not just to you, but to the people you share your life with. Meniere's disease can create a state of being you have never experienced in your life before. This happens not only on a physiological medical textbook level, but an emotional and financial level too. Meniere's can affect not only your general sense of well-being, income, savings, future plans, but your family, friends, and business partnerships.

This is the Meniere Effect. One thing leading to another. It can cause physical changes like hearing loss as well as significant changes to your financial status, workplace and close relationships. Knowing that the Meniere's Effect can happen as part of the condition, means you should put measures in place to limit the negative ripple effects of Meniere's on your everyday life.

First understand that the butterfly does not cause the tornado. Just like Meniere's disease does not cause chaos in your personal and financial life. It's the measures you neglect to address, that cause extra problems while you are suffering with symptoms of Meniere's disease. And this is what this book is about. Once you are aware of the Meniere's Effect, you will be able to cope with the "butterflies" of Meniere's disease.

Whether you worry about your own situation or someone you care about, this book goes to the heart of what we most neglect when suffering with Meniere's and yet what is the most important to us…our personal lives and relationships.

While you manage the disease itself, you must manage to keep chaos out of other parts of your life. When you do this, the ripple effect shifts to a positive one. With a few simple measures in place, you can reduce massive life stress. If you do this, your opportunity to get better quicker, increases dramatically.

People ask me why I write about Meniere's disease now that I am well. The fact is now I have knowledge and I know what it feels like to be in the middle of the Meniere syndrome. Meniere's disease changed the course of my life. And one way to make sense of this dramatic life change is to write about it. Writing has become part of the healing process. The knowledge I gained from living a period of my life with the condition means

I know Meniere's disease as well as my own reflection in the mirror. Managing

Meniere's is something I have had great experience with. The advantage of experiencing something that affects you, is that you understand how it is for other people.

While you are doing all you can to help yourself, you will meet people who are empathetic to sufferers. You will, unfortunately come across people who simply have no idea what it means to suffer from Meniere's disease. And unless they have the condition, they never will understand the impact Meniere's has on living a happy life. These are the people who are not disabled by anything except a closed mind to the plight of others. In fact, one of the reasons I continue to write books on Meniere's is a high court judge wrote that "Meniere's is a mere minor inconvenience." Don't we wish that were true!

This is the sixth self-help book I have written about coping with aspects of Meniere's disease. Many of these books are recommended by ENT Specialists and Audiologists in Australia, and The United Kingdom. Especially the bestselling *Meniere Man Let's Get Better: A Memoir of Meniere's disease*. And the bestselling *Meniere Man and the Astronaut:*

The Self-help Book for Meniere's disease. Other books to help Meniere sufferers are *'Vertigo Vertigo: About Vertigo, About Dizziness and What You Can Do About It'*. *'Meniere Man Meditations* (CD): *Relaxing Healing Meditations for Meniere's disease sufferers'*. *'Meniere Man and the Butterfly: How to Minimize the Meniere Effect On Family, Money, Lifestyle, Dreams and You'*. *'Meniere Man In The Kitchen. Recipes that helped me get over Meniere's: Delicious nutritious low salt recipes from our family kitchen'*.

I've written Meniere Man and the Butterfly because if I had been aware of the Meniere Effect I could have saved myself and my family a lot of grief and loss. You must have the infrastructure of a good action plan to be strong and steady through this time of uncertainty. Not just for you, but for your family as well.

THE DIAGNOSTIC EFFECT

When I was first diagnosed with Meniere's disease, I had no idea of the effect it would have on my life. I can still remember the ENT specialist saying "You have Meniere's disease. And there is nothing we can do about it. The best advice I can give you is to stay away from stress". I was forty-six. A business executive with a young family; my beautiful wife, two children, one at school and one at university, mortgages, a stack of bills and five cats.

The diagnosis was so unexpected it came as a huge shock to all of us. But that was just the beginning. That diagnosis was the butterfly and the effect would drastically change my life to where I am sitting writing this book today. From having three water-front properties, two cars, and children in the middle of their education and money derived from more than twenty-five years of hard slog developing a business. In less than five years, I went from a wealthy self-made man to Meniere Man, an author and man of small means! I only complain occasionally! I have, together with my family, had to structure a new life and it's not all bad, but it is not the one we planned and dreamed of.

As soon as you are diagnosed with Meniere's you have to make decisions about work and finances. When you are ill you tend to make hurried decisions you later regret.

When symptoms got so bad that I couldn't function in my business, I relied on an Income Continuance Policy which seemed to be the right thing to do at the time. The insurance company did not go the distance! It happens!

Instead of relying on an outside provider, I should have sat down with my partner in the weeks following diagnosis. We should have talked about how we could make a few adjustments to our living situation without the support of the insurance company. Instead, by relying on an Insurance Policy instead of "paddling my own outrigger" the Meniere Effect happened with dramatic consequences. The effect on work, career, money, saving and future plans was shattering.

But all is not lost as the saying goes. A fat wallet has been replaced by a bigger heart. I changed country, patterns and habits for the better, I believe. I can call no place home but I am at home everywhere.

Do I wish I had my old life back? Yes I do. Money and solid assets gave me a secure feeling. And it gave me freedom to travel. Not having money has meant that I am living in a third world country in my early sixties. Something only artists and writers do. So that is what I have become. I paint and I write. Life is decidedly interesting.

When I had money, I would have stayed at the Metropole Hotel in a five star luxury suite. I would not have found Da Tuong Street, with its food alley and songbirds in bamboo cages. I would have been another tourist on a one week tour of Hanoi and not a permanent foreign resident, with visa extensions filling my red rubber stamped passport.

I wouldn't have met Vinh, the young

man who taught me his language, or his crazy brother who has outbursts of shouting just before it rains. I would have had less community. I would have had more sleep. Hanoi is a noisy place. I would have come here as a tourist for a few days, instead of this self-imposed exile to find a cheaper place to live and write.

I would have eaten breakfast like a tourist. An almond croissant and espresso. Then wiped the crumbs with a starched white napkin, instead of sitting as I will do this morning, on a blue plastic stool, huddled next to any stranger.

I watch the woman as she pours hot chicken stock onto chopped cilantro and cuts pieces of goose with scissors; as she dips rice noodles, transparent as glass, into the steaming broth. I always tell her to leave out the salt and MSG, then I add a squeeze of lime and slice of chili. That is my breakfast.

I used to eat toasted muesli and plums stewed with orange juice or bitter marmalade on homemade whole-wheat toast with a cup of Darjeeling tea. Or scrambled eggs with four rashers of crisp grilled bacon. That was breakfast. The butterfly flapped its wings and

Meniere's changed my life.

I was unaware of how Meniere's would drastically change my life. Looking back, I wish I had understood the ripple on affect of Meniere's disease. I would not have lost millions in assets. It should never have happened. Neither should you lose anything more than some hearing capacity from Meniere's.

How the butterfly of diagnosis will affect you is personal and subjective. But there are basic patterns to long term illness and suggestions here that can help you cope with. Share the information in this book with your family and friends, so they can understand something of what you are going through.

Had the diagnosis not happened, the butterfly not flapped its wings; this period of my life might have been vastly different. But then I would not be writing this book to you. I write in the hope that you will see the butterflies of good health and fortune in the following chapters.

THE FIRST EFFECTS OF MENIERE'S

When my daughter was studying medicine, I was awed by the thick volumes of text books she studied. The muscles and bones of the body in Latin terms. Thousands of headings and entries for diseases named after the people who discovered them. Just like a our French doctor, Meniere, who first identified the inner ear balance disorder, back in 1861. More than a hundred years later, research into the cause and cure, is still happening. Now I know some Latin as well, but Meniere's is hard to decipher. And at times so is life.

Yesterday I was thinking about people I know. So many of my friends have had to make changes to their jobs or plans because of illness. Cancer. Lupus. MS. Parkinson's and more. It seems, just by being human, sooner or later in life you get an affliction.

Some have diseases diagnosed from childhood. One of my friends has to cope with a disease of the longest German name. Another friend is battling Lupus, named after a wolf.

Our weakness and fragility happens because we are human. We take familiarity for permanence. Yet our life, in the greater picture of humanity, is less than the snap of forefinger and thumb. It is vital to make the most of life, in sickness and in health, whatever illness card is drawn for us. Life is experiential.

When you are sick, *"don't give up to it"*. This is just what my wife wrote to her father in an email yesterday. He was diagnosed with cancer last week. We are vulnerable by our flesh and blood and not alone in our suffering.

Before I was diagnosed with Meniere's disease, I was in good health. An annual medical determined I was physically well. I felt great. I was a high energy and drive kind of guy. Business results showed a guy doing exceptionally well. An executive at the peak of his career. Relationship wise, family was everything in my life. A happy marriage, two great kids; a family that worked, played and stayed together.

Our business survived the share market crash, but there were signs that I was heading for a physical crash. Other people saw small changes in my health and demeanour before I did. I think I was too busy to notice. I write in detail about this in my book, *Let's Get Better, a Memoir of Meniere's disease.*

The Christmas vacation before I was diagnosed was the most telling. We were on vacation at the beach house two hours drive from the city. I was sitting in the sun, shucking scallops that we had dived for that morning. I was caught on video camera looking pale and drawn. My eyes vacant and I seemed preoccupied. It was summer vacation! The sun shining; the Christmas blossom on the native trees; scarlet red against a backdrop of the bluest Pacific Ocean. Volcanic islands on the horizon where I loved to fish for snapper. Come on. Get happy!

But something in the picture was out of normal sync. It was me. I was quiet and mono syllabic. The camera does not lie. It was telling. I was absolutely exhausted. I said to my wife something like, "You know I don't want to wind-down during this break, because I don't feel like I will be able to wind up again." A telling statement.

One year later, I was suffering from the disabling physical symptoms of Meniere's disease. And along with the distress of being unable to manage the symptoms, I felt I was no longer determining the course of my life. Instead I was experiencing the emotional bleakness of waiting for the vertigo monster to come and take me. All my thinking, acting and feeling involved falling into the clutches of acute vertigo attacks. My reality was intense fear.

When you can't cope with physical symptoms, then psychological symptoms get in the act. Then you'll find you can no longer cope with life's ups and downs. You'll develop anxiety, fear and depression.

In the beginning Meniere's feels destructive and there seems nothing can be done to fix it. You wake up with it. You go to bed with it. Then you realize it is not just about Meniere's. It's about your life and what is happening to it. Unlike a headache, you can't take two pain relievers and feel better half an hour later. And it's not like a bad back, which goes away after physiotherapy. Meniere's can feel like you have something else onboard your body. The feeling of having something wrong, takes up serious space in your mind.

When I was diagnosed with Meniere's disease I was unable to find more than a folded A4 pamphlet from the reading rack in the ENT specialist's office. It held no answers. I was used to getting a cold or flu, spending a few days resting and then be up and back to normal. But this was something a bowl of chicken soup couldn't fix. I didn't know where to begin. And the truth is, I was feeling too overwhelmed to begin to try. You may also be at this point right now.

This point of inaction is the twilight zone where you are too stunned to move in any direction and the inertia means you are stuck, waiting for an attack. You have no idea when the next vertigo attack will happen. Or do we?

If you formulate a plan to manage your condition, almost immediately you'll begin to set a course for a better life. It's a course of action. Having a plan is like making your own personal map. You start to navigate the condition and to understand where you are going. You become the orienteer rather than the disorientated one. A plan will give you immense courage and enhance your ability to heal. Making a plan and acting on it is how you move forward to better health with Meniere's disease. You can begin to make a personal plan by first identifying the level of vertigo you are experiencing right now.

THE EFFECT OF VERTIGO SYMPTOMS

Not enough is known about Meniere's disease. And symptoms like vertigo and tinnitus can differ from moment to moment. You may be one of the lucky ones with hardly any symptoms to speak of. Or you may be like me...where the symptoms went from bad to acute in a few months.

Light Vertigo

If you are extremely lucky, dizziness will not affect your normal life at all. But take care if you are at this point. Some people start off with light symptoms and don't make changes, like reducing salt intake or stress levels. They carry on as normal and put up with symptoms. This is when dizziness causes you to stop what you are doing for a while. But the dizziness soon passes and you can get back to what you were doing.

This pattern of Meniere's was exactly where it began for me. At this point I could still do my job, drive a car, travel, and do anything I felt like. I actually didn't change anything I was doing. I was still socially reliable, so I never had to cancel anything. I went out for dinner, stayed up late, and drank wine and coffee. I could plan an activity, and never have to change my plans because of dizziness. But after a few months the intensity of the dizziness increased to moderate vertigo.

Moderate Vertigo

I had to change plans and make allowances for the dizziness. I only just managed to work, socialize and drive a car. I had to change most my plans to accommodate Meniere's symptoms into my activities. Meniere's symptoms were not easy to ignore at this point. So I went from Meniere's not initially affecting my lifestyle in the beginning, to having to accommodate bouts of rotational spinning vertigo. I managed for a year like this. Meniere's at this point interrupted my life. But I still did not put management measures in place.

Severe Vertigo

My levels of distress became worse. I was trying to be normal. I ended up suffering with the acute symptoms of Meniere's every day. I could no longer do my job; I could drive the car sometimes; I could no longer do everything I wanted to do in a day. It took a huge amount of effort to hold everything together. The random nature of frequent attacks meant I barely made it through each day. I had to limit or cut down activities to save energy. And I did not communicate with the significant people in my life about how distressing and impossible my situation was becoming.

When symptoms of Meniere's disease start impacting on your life and your essential activities get limited down, you have to acknowledge that Meniere's has become a disabling condition. Then you have to talk to the people in your life about what is happening to you. How you feel does affect them.

This stage is the worst degree of disability. For the first time in your life you may be frightened about your ability to get back to normal. I know I was. And I felt that I was on my own. When you are in this state it is hard to respond to others and explain exactly how it is. Because your energies and focus are directed inward toward healing and controlling panic. At this point, when the bouts of vertigo were relentless, Meniere's, for me was like a black hole.

THE BLACK HOLE EFFECT

A black hole, as we know it, is a place in space where gravity pulls so much that even light can't get out. Anything that gets too close to a black hole gets swallowed up. The black hole swallows starlight. For me, Meniere's vertigo is a metaphor for the black hole by the feeling it creates within your physical world.

You are doing life as you know it with all its intricacy. Then the symptom of acute vertigo happens and you tumble into endless hyperspace. A black hole is the end of thoughts. A black hole is no control. No agreement. Meniere's is against one's will. Not something you would wish even on your worst enemy, Meniere's disease is a place not anywhere anyone would want to go. In the early days of

Meniere's, when you can't comprehend what is happening, there feels like there isn't even a pinprick of hope in the dark tunnel of hours, days and weeks that go by.

Just as a black hole in space can suck energy out of the universe, the confrontational physical nature of Meniere's seems to suck out your confidence and your sense of worth. Even your certainty that you can survive is something you question. At what point will you, no longer be you? What do you have to cling to, to hold on to? And then what? If the ground on which we stand isn't safe, then what?

When you look at Meniere's, it has a drastic range of sensations, none of them pleasant. From the virtual uneasiness, and cold sweat dread as vertigo approaches; as it gives way to nervousness, dizziness, nausea, vertigo, anxiety, panic, terror, and dread; to the overwhelming sense of personal disembodiment as you live in the spinning black hole of Meniere's.

When one vertigo attack is followed by another, with a vengeance, your personal universe shrinks. Each day is a challenge. You find yourself living in the in-between space. The gap between attacks is the only place you can squeeze into. This becomes life as you know it. You are grateful for any respite. To be not under attack. To be left alone, is enough.

I realized that Meniere's not only affected my physical body but Meniere's affected my mental head-space. Meniere's becomes the yardstick of your existence, the thing you measure life activities against. Meniere's becomes the filter you run things through, the decider, the enemy within, and the authority you ask. The why, how, when and all of it, can dominate your waking day.

When vertigo is as severe as this, events are often confused and the sense of time is distorted. At these times, we retreat into ourselves. So recognize that you need help at this stage. You need a support network but you will need help from people closest to you to put that together. Depending on what you need, ask someone to make appointments with advisors such as psychologists, financial advisors and support groups. Go together with your partner or family member so everyone is aware and informed. The more you know and understand, the more light it shines on the dark space of Meniere's.

From personal experience of suffering the condition and working my way back to a healthy, fit and active life again, I can tell you there is a light at the end of a dark tunnel. It was during the first six months of experiencing the black hole of vertigo, that I began to work on changing my lifestyle to work towards better health. Despite the vertigo, I found space between the attacks. It was between attacks that I went for a walk, cooked dinner, sat in the sun, and did the gym. I found it was possible to do activities incrementally.

When you focus on the time between vertigo attacks, it is surprising how much time you can find there. The more you use the in-between space, the less of a black hole you experience. Find those spaces, get active and you'll find you are no longer stuck but you're moving forward towards better health.

THE EFFECT OF INFORMATION

There is a saying knowledge is power. I'd say information is the best medicine. You can do this by gaining information about Meniere's disease from your doctor and by reading books and observing your own experience with Meniere's.

The more you find out about Meniere's disease, the more in control you will feel, the less anxiety, fear and stress you will have. And since stress and anxiety are known to be triggers for vertigo attacks, you'll start to manage the condition.

Everybody is different. There are still no answers to what causes Meniere's but there is more information of how to manage it. No one knows for sure the how and why exactly, but the overall contribution of the collective, sufferers, doctors, specialists and researchers, means there is greater information available to help you overcome the Meniere Effect.

Personal accounts are invaluable too because they give a perspective of an insiders point of view. No medical text can do this. Everyone is different. Not everyone fits into the patient mode of treatments, medication and surgical options. Sometimes we prefer to look at an insider's point of view as well. To find people who have been exactly where we are and have come out the other side smiling.

The Meniere Effect means you will need to make some changes in your life. I have come to understand the bottom-line basics of physiological and psychological aspects of the condition. When you understand the condition and what is happening to you, you'll be able to manage Meniere's. The more you know, the more you can figure the puzzle of the disease and how the pieces fit for you in your life. Use information and make plans for your wellness. This is will get you to the place you want to be.

If you want to understand the inside out of vertigo attacks, you may want to read *Verti-*

go Vertigo: About Vertigo About Dizziness and What You Can Do About it. It explains what happens and how to cope during each stage of a vertigo attack. This information helps take the fear out of the attacks. The less fear you have, the more you take control of the spinning dervish. As you find ways to cope, you'll find each vertigo attack becomes less and less distressing. You will start to put activities back in your life and you'll feel less limited. You will know how to live your life between attacks and the space between attacks will get bigger. Your life will become less restricted by Meniere's. You will feel like you are beginning to get your life back. Remember Meniere's is not terminal and the attacks will pass.

You can find out about Meniere's from professional sources. In the back of this book, there is a list of resources for Meniere's disease. And support networks. The professional overviews give you the medical findings on medical procedures and up to date treatments available such as vestibular balance training techniques. You can find out what psychological affects you can expect from having long term conditions such as Meniere's disease.

The best way to use new information is to apply things that resonate for you. Your own healing process is instinctive. When I was diagnosed, I became focused on doing balancing activities. Although each activity used different equipment, they had something in common. They all required balance. I learned weight lifting, snowboarding, surfing, windsurfing and core balance training. Now I can look back and see that this was my self-healing instinct working, although I had no idea at the time.

I worked on my core at home with a fitness ball. The fitness ball is unstable, so training on it helps strengthen your stabilizing muscles. What is your core? Like the cables of steel that hold up a bridge, your core is the support system for your body. It stabilizes your spine and connects your lower and upper extremities. The core is your center of balance, so it plays an important role in helping you maintain your balance. Strengthening the core muscles of spine, pelvis, shoulders, back and hip muscles helped improve my balance and equilibrium. I had less of that unsteady feeling you get following an attack. It also gave me physical confidence. Which in turn gave me renewed optimism.

Years later, I read that if you do balance compensating activities, then it really helps the vertigo issue. In fact, there are vestibular clinics now who have targeted programs for rehabilitation balance exercises. My learning balance activities is an example of how instinct helps you determine what you need.

Learn as much as you can. For every disease there are self-help management strategies. They can be small and simple steps you take. If you had heart disease, for example, you would self-treat by cutting down fat in your diet. Meniere's symptoms can be self managed too. The more information you have, the more you can do to help yourself, the less threatening Meniere's is. Following the self -help suggestions in this book will help you be pro-active. You'll be more in control of managing your symptoms and life in general.

If you have Meniere books, pass them on to friends and family. Educate others around you about the condition. If you can't find information yourself, ask others to help you. I needed information on vitamin and mineral supplements but I was unable to scroll on the computer without feeling dizzy. So I asked my wife to do the searching for me.

She found a local health food home-store in the yellow pages of the phone directory. I wish I could remember the name of the store owner to thank her for all the advice she gave us. People cross your path at times when you need them. She and my wife talked for many hours on the phone. First they figured from type of work I did, that stress and long hours may have depleted my adrenals. So the boxes of vitamins C and E arrived. Bottles and plastic containers filled with gel capsules and tablets. The kitchen looked like a dispensary.

By taking the vitamins and mineral regularly I felt I was doing something to help myself. My wife felt like she was empowered as well. The two women were absolutely right. This was the beginning of an extensive vitamin plan and strategy for wellness. To see my detailed vitamin plan, look in Meniere Man *Let's Get Better*.

Be pro-active. Learn as many positive strategies as you can to help reduce Meniere's symptoms, manage Meniere's attacks and regain a sense of balance and power in your life.

Pick up your pen. Keep a diary. I did for the first year. Information is a key factor in recovering your sense of equilibrium. The more personal information you have the better it is for you. Be a careful observer and pay attention to what you write down in your diary. You are looking for clues. Look for patterns of cause and affect. You are matching possible causes with triggers. When you know your triggers, you can find answers which go a long way to help prevent attacks in the first place.

The more you understand about Meniere's disease, the how, the why, the when of vertigo attacks, each attack will stop feeling like such a big deal. Over time, managing a vertigo attack will become second nature. You'll find you can begin to function in the world again, despite having Meniere's.

When life deals you Meniere's, it's an unexpected challenge. Talk to your doctor about how it is for you. Ask what treatments your doctor or specialist recommends. Find out what medications can relieve or even stop a vertigo attack. Ask how effective they are. Read the small print for any medication the doctor has put you on. Know what to expect when you are taking medicines for Meniere's. Do they have side affects or complications? Be bold. Ask for a second opinion. Find out as much as you can about treatment options. This puts you in control. If you are on medication, ask how long it will be before you will notice results. Ask for appropriate help. It is not a personal weakness to ask for assistance.

Understand how diet affects the symptoms. Ask for a referral to see a dietician. Talk to a dietician. Find out how simple changes in your diet can help reduce Meniere's disease symptoms. Get help to plan your eating. Learn what foods are off and on the menu.

When your diet is sorted, you have one less thing to worry about. You are doing all you can to gain a sense of control. Then move on to bigger action plans like balancing programs or meditation. Then move on to even bolder plans...the sky has no limit.

THE MAPPING EFFECT ON WELLNESS

Meniere's can make it hard to live life effectively. Having the condition can significantly interfere with your ability to maintain healthy relationships with partners, spouses and others. You will need outside help.

Apart from this book, and other books you read, and the information from your doctors and specialists...there is a point where you come into the equation. You get sick of being sick! You start to look for creative ways to put the experience of living back into your life. It is up to you to try. If you feel something resonates with you, then try it.

To get a sense of respite from Meniere's I looked for ways of taking time-out. Often the focus of alternative therapies worked well. I was lucky enough to have time for regular massages and tried other forms of therapies outlined in *Let's Get Better*. They act like a map to help you locate yourself in relation to your situation. Trying different therapies helps you overcome the displacement and depression which Meniere's can cause.

Get the support of a therapist. They can help you deal with stress and emotions. I talked to a therapist who used to listen when I was depressed, frustrated and down- and even when I was just feeling happy! Accepting emotions, expressing or sharing your emotions, helps you cope and feel better about things.

Just talking about how Meniere's makes you feel, helps a lot. You can join Meniere's support groups in your area and meet other people with Meniere's disease. The main thing is to find support and talk to people you can trust enough to share on an intimate level. When you talk it helps clarify your feelings and thinking. This helps with your action plans for wellness.

When you understand Meniere's, share what you know with close friends or family.

They can understand how you feel and how it affects your life. You help each other understand what is going on. The healing affect goes both ways. You don't have to find someone who is a professional, just someone who will listen to how you are feeling in a kind, caring and non-judgmental way. Love is a healer. You can even talk to the cat!

THE MENIERE EFFECT ON YOUR MIND

Know that when you are struggling with Meniere's you are not alone. Millions of people suffer from the affects of Meniere's disease. Some are yet to find out what the attacks of vertigo, nausea and vomiting are. Others are hearing the news right now from their doctor that they have got Meniere's disease. The diagnosis of a disorder that has such confrontational symptoms brings with it a complex bag of physical and psychological difficulties, such as anxiety, fear, and a protracted period of suffering from the stress of having the condition in the first place. Being diagnosed with any illness or disease has been recognized to give the sufferer a sense of loss and grief.

The emotional trauma of Meniere's is caused by loss of a valued level of functioning, the ability to stay balanced. Balance is our important sixth sense on so many levels. Losing the certainty of balance creates personal emotional pain. At times this becomes overwhelming as Meniere's disease and everything to do with it, engulfs your life.

When you have a vertigo attack, you immediately lose balance competency. And the more attacks of vertigo you have, the more the general feeling of certainty goes from your life. All the plans you had for the future seem to vanish. All the plans and goals you made for the direction of a future, seen irrelevant, when you are lying down spinning out.

There are stages of coping with Meniere's disease. When you have just been diagnosed you can feel particularly confused and vulnerable. Your life as you know it is about to change whether you want it to or not. So a sense of powerlessness happens. Maybe for the first time in your life, you are worried about your health and how it will impact on your future plans and dreams.

A sense of loss is a big factor in how you

can feel with Meniere's. You lose your equilibrium and a feeling that all is right in your world. The intensity of vertigo attacks fluctuates day to day. At times, vertigo drags you far away from your recognizable self. It may seem that you are living only to experience vertigo.

When you have Meniere's, you may find it hard to relax, you can feel drained easily. You don't sleep that well. And you feel on edge. When you feel anxious all the time, you can feel an overwhelming sense that Meniere's is all pervasive in your life. When you feel anxious and worried, it can be debilitating. Meniere's can trigger a sense of anxiety that you can't seem to shake.

You lose a sense of hope that you will ever recover a normal life again. You can lose personal feelings too…a sense of well-being, self belief and self-sufficiency. You need to be aware that this can lead to depression. Sleeping a lot, crying, grumpiness, anger, sadness and anxiety may be symptoms of depression.

Depression and stress are common as you try to balance the realities of dealing with Meniere's symptoms and coping with work, friends, family and everyday life. If you are suffering with depression, then professional help is what you need to get.

I met a round the world Yachtswoman once and she told me no one has ever been seasick on her boat. The reason is a simple one. She always tells people where they are going and how long it will take to get there. One of the things that cause humans the greatest stress is the unknown.

Most of our natural world has a rhythm. The season. The passing of time. Months. Years. The rising and setting of the sun. Most of us are born like clockwork. Gestation time up, nine months and we are ready to go.

What holds us back in life are the uncertainties. By nature we need to have a handle on things. We thrive on knowing exactly what is going on. Why? Because then we can make plans. Plans move us forward in our lives. They give us both a sense of momentum and a sense of fulfilment when we reach our goals.

You can feel your life is all about Meniere's and Meniere's has taken over your normal life in every respect. But in reality, while Meniere's is a confrontational condition only. You can take steps to enjoy living your life and feeling happy despite having the condition.

To manage feelings of anxiety and fear, make a list of the situations that causes you the most anxiety. Are any of the fears associated with Meniere's irrational e.g. fear of suddenly spinning out in a public when in reality, the likelihood of that happening is not as great because you would have warning symptoms before that happened. And even if you did, it's likely that people around you would help you out. There is always a forward momentum to life and that's what you have to realize and tune into.

When you plan and action your plans you will go from limited and restricted to being back to a normal sense of well-being and feelings of productivity. The gap in between may be a journey in itself, but keep in mind that you are not going backwards with this.

Keep in mind that the early days are the worst, when you may have believed that your life would be one bad vertigo attack after another. Leave the fears back there. The more you understand, the further you move away from the first awful months.

Don't expect to like the compromises you

need to make in order to manage your symptoms. Just know that changes in life style have to be made. But keep in mind you are taking control and you are making the changes. This re-focus makes you look for greater and more positive things you can do.

If you are a perfectionist by nature, then look at setting realistic goals and outcomes. And while you are learning new things like yoga, focus on what you can do. Keep your humor up. Not being able to do the perfect down dog is no big deal. You don't have to be top dog anymore. Be less hard on yourself.

Take time out from activities. Take a break. Find the new Meniere activity time. I had time limits on everything I did. Like ten minutes on the computer. Stop. Walk ten minutes. Stop. Do things incrementally. Stop before you get overwhelmed. Learn to recognize the built in stop sign you have. Don't go past it.

Learn to unlearn any habits of keeping going and over riding how your body feels. Check in with yourself like a friend would. How are you doing? How's it going? Recognize when it's time for a break.

THE MENIERE EFFECT ON YOUR PARTNER AND FAMILY

You might not be the only one who feels emotional about your illness. Family and friends often have an increase in anxiety. Partners especially, as they have full responsibility for looking after your life together. And if children are involved, seeing that children's lives can go on as normally as possible. Don't forget the children. Help them to understand why you suddenly disappear out of the room. Why you aren't always there to kick a ball around or help with homework.

You know, I forgot to explain to my kids and family about how it was for me. I some how expected them to instinctively know. It would have been so much better if I had the knowledge about all aspects of the Meniere Effect and explained to people what was going on. But I didn't. I didn't want to show weakness and vulnerability. I tried to act normal. But to partners and close family I had become remote, as I had stopped communicating fully.

Partners and family feel a need, sometimes an obligation, to be highly supportive of you. They can worry about you so much their anxiety can be de-energizing. Partners often respond to your illness by doing too much and giving you a lot of attention. Unfortunately, when you are suffering acute bouts of vertigo, you can't appreciate these signs of love.

Sometimes partners can try too much to make things right for you and that they become exhausted. My wife gave up work for eighteen months to be around for me. She did so much research on diet and supplements trying to find the answers. Helping me out eased her sense of loss and change. Helping, she said made watching me suffer easier to manage. Later I said I hardly remembered her being there for me. Can you imagine how her sacrifice felt! I was so ill back then; almost all of my energy was focused on responding to the physical attacks of vertigo. All sense of time and proportion faded. Time blurred, and so did the edges of normal life.

If I was going through Meniere's again I would explain to her that it is not for her to cure me! There is a balance and partners must find it. They can be strong for you but they shouldn't give up their own lives during the time of Meniere's. When someone loves you, they hate seeing you so sick. They tend to think back and feel guilty about things in the past. Did they do something that made you spin out? Did they cook a meal where the ingredients contained salt? Did they cause the argument that stressed you out? Treading eggs-shells is what they do around you.

Partners, once they understand the triggers for Meniere's attacks, can become hyper vigilant and police what you do. They remind you not to do this. Or not do that. They have your best interests at heart but the danger of someone caring is that they can over care and take away your sense of personal choice. They take control and parent you to prevent vertigo attacks. They do this so they don't feel bad seeing you suffer.

When you have Meniere's disease other people's emotions can feel like an extra burden on you. Trying to cope with your own dynamics is difficult but add in your partners worries and it is a serious added burden. Of course how down they feel about it all is not their fault. But it is hard to not feel guilty for causing them emotional pain of the added stress of your disease.

The Meniere Effect happens in relationships. While your partner doesn't suffer symptoms, they do suffer along with you. Your partner can feel as much fear about the future as you do. As well as you, your partner must cope with the fear of an unknown and unknowable future. It is clear that the comfortable patterns of the past have been shattered.

Partners often become tired, exhausted and fed up. They will have periods where they feel not up to dealing with the affects Meniere's has on you. The one's closest to you are most affected by the Meniere's but don't always receive the support and help they need.

Your partner can spend lonely hours worrying about you. They suffer in silence with you. I know my wife tells me she did. Often with no one to talk to because the person they usually talk to, is the one they want to talk about. So it is so important that they have their own network of support.

You can't blame fate or anyone else for your situation. But you may have moments when you think you bought the disease on yourself by lifestyle in some way. At times like this, you need to tell yourself that it is Meniere's disease that introduced the disruption into your life. And you did not cause it. This can make you feel angry.

Feeling angry is a normal part of coping. You can become angry at your situation and direct it towards people you love and care about: your partner, family and friends.

Your partner may feel angry. They may see the changes in their life style as caused by you. If either partner is feeling angry, then it affects both of your emotional well-being. Anger creates a strain on both of you. You can get trapped in anger and it is counter-productive to wellness.

If either of you are feeling angry, then you need to take back control. Working toward a goal together can stop the feelings of anger. This is the basic rule in dealing with anger caused by the situation. You simply focus on what you have together and the personal strengths you each have and make a plan. Talk about this. Express your needs. Are there things you can help each other with? Remember, illness does not just affect you. It can be lonely time and a draining worry for the other person. While they don't suffer the symptoms, they can suffer in silence. So keep talking and expressing feelings and you'll both feel better.

Let your partner know how you are feeling. Take care not to make them feel helpless or guilty because you are feeling that way. If you feel tired or irritable, tell them. If you don't, people will react to your mood. Let people know that you are feeling exhausted. Don't try to hide the fact. If you can keep it real, the lines of communication between you are open.

When you are heard and you take time to listen, even in adversity, all your relationships improve. You will cope better emotionally if you are consciously big-hearted. If you act towards each other in a big hearted way. By sharing interests and compassion, it gives meaning and purpose in life and helps on the road to recovery.

Work as a team; you are on the same side. The main thing for you and your partner to understand is this. You are not the same as the disease. And both of you are committed to getting a life back. Find ways to love nurture and support each other in order to cope with the anxiety and fear Meniere's disease can make you feel.

Keep doing things together. Even if you feel too unreliable. Make a date with each other. Continue to find some pleasure in each day. Plan one activity a day. Going for a walk. Having a drink in a café. Sitting outside in the garden. A movie. Offer mutual support, human touch, hugs, massage and a close physical relationship. You'll find even in the time of Meniere's your relationship will grow. Love in a time of Meniere's.

A sense of humor gets you through. Every experience of love, emotional and physical connection, appreciation, does too. The more you feel like you are living and alive, the better you feel. Love is the most powerful healer of all. To both give and receive it.

THE MENIERE EFFECT ON FRIENDS

Sharing with family and friends is one of life's pleasures. You will find that some friends also tend to give out on you. Some friends may find it too much of a personal struggle to continue to phone you or drop over. I often wonder where good friends go.

You may feel a sense of unfairness and senselessness. Why should you have Meniere's disease. This makes you look at other people around you, friends and colleagues and wonder how come you have this disease; you can envy their normal and unaffected life; when your current situation with Meniere's disease seems unfair. You need support.

You don't need to suffer from Meniere's alone. Surround yourself with people who support you and distance yourself from people who do not want to understand. It is important not to become socially isolated so your life gets smaller and smaller until it takes place in two rooms, the bathroom and the bedroom. And the only person in that room is you.

Do dinner with friends. All this helps you and your partner stay in social contact. It is too easy to turn down invitations. Accept them on the proviso that you may not come. People who care understand this. Don't isolate yourself. And don't let your condition stop you or your partner's social life.

THE MENIERE EFFECT ON YOUR JOB

Many people suffering with disease try to keep their condition secret. I can put my hand up here! But trying to hide a condition can cause its own problems. It is hard, if not impossible to keep Meniere's undisclosed for long. There is no need to deny to that you have Meniere's or to pretend to others that you are fine, when you are not.

For me, I became unreliable and my work suffered. I was still working the same hours and didn't take time off, because I had not informed anyone that I needed too. In fact I didn't know that I needed the time off myself. When you explain the condition, as I discovered later, you will be surprised at how accepting people are. If you are willing to ask for help and you have a wide support network, you'll have an easier time.

Explaining the facts of Meniere's helps, employers and business partners understand what you're capable of. It allows them to appreciate your capabilities - the person you are, a partner, a talent, a contributor, an intelligent person, someone who makes a difference. Not just a Meniere sufferer.

Practice being self-reflective and look at your personal talents and qualities. Think of things you can do with these qualities. When I had Meniere's I started to take notes about Meniere's disease. How it was for me. In that way I could put positive energy back into the world.

At the time I didn't realize that would be more than six books on Meniere's disease. When you put your personal talents, knowledge and experience out there, it can help others. You can do this within business, family, friends, or with Meniere's self-help groups.

THE MENIERE EFFECT ON FINANCES

How can you best protect what you have right now from the financial erosion that can happen with illness? Medical bankruptcy is a real threat when someone is ill. No one is ever prepared for this. Unless your mattress is bulging with cash, chances are you will need to formulate a new plan for your finances.

Look for and plan for a fall back position if things go bad. The fall back position is not necessarily claiming on Income Continuance. Insurance security is the absence of awareness of danger. So the famous Ancient Greek Aristotle wrote centuries ago. I believe that may be true today. Certainly from my personal experience of insurance not being there for the long haul. It pays to read the smallest of the small print. Often family are the only ones you can truly trust to help with advice and support should you need some. See what you can do as a family collective if you need serious help.

While you need to make adjustments to protect your assets, take care not to rush into making major decisions. Never feel forced to make changes you may regret at a later date. When you are suffering with acute vertigo attacks, you may not make good decisions because you are not physically and mentally up to it. So for any decision that will have long term ramifications, you should seek financial advice. Then take this advice and give yourself and your family time to decide what is the right course of action.

Never rush into a knee-jerk reaction because of Meniere's. Always take your time to think and contemplate. Examples of changes that can impact on your future are: moving house, leaving your employment, selling shares in your business, leaving your partner or cashing up investments. These are just some examples of financial changes that need careful consideration.

Looking back if I were to give you a piece of advice, I would say this: avoid instigating radical change. The kind of change that creates disruption, chaos, wrong decisions and regrets. Meniere's is not a reason for a big shake-up of life as you know it. It is a well-known fact that a big change creates stress in your life. You have enough stress with the diagnosis. You want to avoid adding any stressful event to the list. So think of making incremental changes where you need too. Make adjustments to the lifestyle framework you already have in place.

If you have worked in your job for the past twelve years and are happy there, do you need to quit? Not necessarily. Ask yourself, can I adjust my workload or job spec, take more breaks. Take some sick days or the holidays you have earned. Everyone around you can help.

Making adjustments and adapting is not something you have to do on your own. Give people information on Meniere's. Let people know how you are feeling. Sharing knowledge and talking, you can figure out opportunities together. Your main job is to work on wellness strategies and conserving your personal energy. Allow people around you to help you with the adapting! You have other things to look after.

The last thing you or your partner need is worry about finances. So take a look. See what you can do. I am now a great believer in being a self-sufficient as you can. Make your own preparations to cope. Are there any practical solutions you can do to counter the affect of having one of you down or out of the normal work force with days off sick. Can your partner take charge of finances? Increased doctor bills, audiologists, extra vitamins and alternative treatments can impact the family budget. What practical steps do you need to put in place to avoid financial blow-out, yet at the same time allow you treatments you need.

Often adjustments in living styles (cutting down on surplus needs and expenses) are extremely difficult to do as you have all been living this way for sometime. Changing the status quo is difficult. It is a time to spend less, get rid of things you don't need, a second car, household employees: the gardener, the cook or cleaner.

On a monthly budget level accept a little less and buy yourself peace of mind. Make do with what you have. Make do with a little less. Wants, desires and must haves and not the same as needs. Recognize the different between practical consumer items and surplus material ones. You can fatten your wallet when you are not working by cutting down your spending.

So as soon as you are given a diagnosis of Meniere's, take notice. You will need to make substantial plans. Talk to your personal banker and financial advisors and colleagues. Talk to heath care givers, councillors and your doctor. Assess the situation and put measures in place. Get a bigger financial safety net.

THE MENIERE EFFECT ON YOUR ENERGY

Energy is a problem when you have Meniere's. It is hard to get a surplus of energy reserves. You can feel drained and tired before you realize it. There is no energy to waste.

How does energy get wasted? You know yourself. If you argue, feel angry or harbor resentment or stress out, you can feel exhausted. These emotions waste energy and wear you out. You need to be emotionally efficient. If you are wasting energy, you just have to stop. Walk away or do something else. Make more friends than enemies and choose your battles. If you engage in conflict you may win the argument but more likely end up a casualty of a vertigo attack.

Think of daily energy as a point system. When you are acutely sick, maybe you feel like you have an energy level on a scale of two out of ten. But after a couple of days of rest your energy levels maybe 7 out of 10. *A tip for energy counting;* the more you do in increments the more energy you will gain. For example, washing the car may be a drain of 2, half hour rest gain 4, so you are ahead by 2. A full car wash maybe a deficit of 5, half hour rest gain 4, equals deficit of 1.

I just want you to think about not doing everything, as it will deplete you and then you stay in that exhausted zone and feel like it's all too much. You need to pay attention to how you feel. If you feel like you have more energy, get going and do things. But don't go for broke go in small increments. The trick is not to drain yourself. Stop before you feel like you have had enough. Let other people finish the job.

You may be halfway through washing the car or cooking a meal. You can suddenly feel like you have had enough. Try to recognize the before "I've had enough" even if you are halfway through a task, stop. Ask someone else to finish it. You are in conservation mode for your energy resources. You have to ask someone to help you at that point. Some people find asking for help as difficult as saying no. You have to learn to ask for help.

Asking for help was not the first choice me. I would rather do everything myself. Allowing people to help you is an art form. There is a grace to it that must be learned. You need to practice asking for help. The reason is that people are not mind-readers. Unless you ask someone to help you, they see you doing something and think you are o.k.

The benefit of asking for help is that people around you know that you are not a martyr. So they trust that you know when to stop and conserve energy. Then they know you can look after yourself in that way. Also no one will nag you or remind you to stop doing this or that. Asking someone for help when you need to is not a weakness or failure.

If you have a hard time asking for help, consider what you would do if you were o.k. and a friend of yours had Meniere's. You would just do it. So the point here is be as kind to yourself as you would to your friends. If asking for help is a skill you have, then you will have more energy.

When you are not drained of energy you build up energy reserves. And your body will use this store of energy for self healing. You need to conserve energy to help yourself. Recover your energy levels through rest, mediation, yoga, laughter, smiling and thinking postively. The higher your energy levels the more you can do for your health. You need to conserve energy for self healing.

THE EFFECT OF LIMITLESS THINKING

If you let Meniere's become the focus of your life - it surely will. And that is limited thinking. It's easy to have this happen as in the beginning all the firsts happen to you. Your first vertigo attack, the first time you saw the specialist, the first time you read about the condition. The first time you said no to a cup of coffee.

Everyone has a life pattern - a personal way of living life. From the time you get out of bed, shower, go for a run or a walk, and make coffee, read the newspaper. Doing life your way. Why should being diagnosed with Meniere's make you make big changes to the life you enjoy? It shouldn't.

Just because the smallest bone in your body, the cochlear bone is giving you symptoms, it doesn't mean that the pleasures you have in your life should stop. You can even keep the same routine going. But you have to adapt. The run may be a walk for a while. The morning coffee...a decaffeinated brew. You read the paper when you feel like it. You make incremental adjustments and then you can re-adjust these later. As your symptoms improve, the decaffeinated coffee can go back to being your morning espresso again.

So think about making temporary changes. Nothing is fixed or set. You are on control. You keep substituting one thing for another, whether in your cooking you substitute salt for herbs, caffeine for decaffeinated, relaxing for overworking, doing things for others to making time for yourself. Listen to your body and you make adjustments as you feel you need to. It's a personal situation. The main thing is you're in control.

Even when you have acute bouts of vertigo, you can be in control as you read in *Vertigo Vertigo*. Make some adjustments and you can do mostly everything you did before the diagnosis. Adapt to the illness but don't give up your life to Meniere's. If you can do that, your life moves forward. O.K you still have the condition, but it doesn't take over your life. Survival of the fittest is about adapting to the situation. You choose the changes you make. Meniere's shouldn't control you. You must stay in control of you life.

When you make choices for better health, you are not missing out on anything. You are working towards having even better health than you had before, by the choices you make. On the simplest level, you throw away the salt shaker and reduce salt in your diet. But you don't go without flavour. You add in more herbs to replace the salt and your meals taste better than before, you enrich your diet. Even this one adaptation has a positive effect on your whole body.

Having Meniere's means you will have to make some adjustments; from your diet, your fitness, your vitamins and mineral regime, your stress management and personal energy conservation to your finance and work situation. But see if you can work within the framework you have. Think in terms of adjustments as adapting elements in your work, home, friends, family, finances, diet and fitness, rather than making massive change.

You are likely to have gained expertise and resilience in other aspects of life that you can apply to coping with Meniere's disease. Experience of mastery and success, goal-oriented striving. These are all skills you can apply to getting better and overcoming the Meniere Effect. All this helps overcome the displacement depression of chronic physical illness.

In order to prevent Meniere's dominating you life, you need to be careful about the care you take to manage Meniere's. Every time you do something to help yourself, you are reminding yourself that you have a condition. Which if you're not careful can become the 24/7 occupation.

When Meniere's is constantly in your mind, you need to put things back in perspective. And forget about Meniere's for a while. Keep up with friends. Read a book. Distract yourself. Watch a movie. Go out for a drink. Read the morning paper in the cafe. Work out at the gym. Paint. Do yoga. Meditate. Swim. Shop. Cook. Garden. Walk in nature. Fish. Go to the beach. Listen to the birds. Listen to music. Call a friend. Watch a sunset. Take photographs. Write. Play with a child. Throw a ball to the dog. Breathe in the salt air of an ocean. Sit in the sun. Read to your kids. Peel an orange. Stroke a cat. Simple things in life here.

You can reduce the emotional impact of vertigo and accompanying anxiety and fear by doing more of what you personally love. To feel o.k. within yourself, while having Meniere's disease, you have to value yourself as a person. Getting a sense of wellness in your life is about giving yourself options. The more experiences you can gain mastery over. The more you create and sustain a sense of wellness, despite having Meniere's.

In all my books, I say, you can't wait until you feel better to start working towards better health. You must do things when you don't feel like doing anything! Just a little at a time. As soon as you can get up in the morning, get dressed and go for a small walk. If you feel woozy and dizzy, take a friend. But do it.

You must do everything you can to stimulate your nerves of balance and get oxygen flowing in your blood. Walking is the basic start. Add to that. But whatever you do, only stay in bed for as long as you have to. Even after an attack, get going again. Honestly even a walk to the sofa is better than isolating in bed.

My recommendation for Meniere's is to make your expectations un-realistic. Yes, that's right un-realistic! The most important aspect of making expectations un-realistic is to expand your boundaries. Un-realistic may be going for a walk, when you feel that you can't, or maybe, learn to windsurf.

Ever diminishing circles are a reality of chronic illness. As your expectations decrease so does your activity. Until the edge of the bed or sofa is your boundary. Check in with yourself to find out what you want to do. Not what you should do. Make personal time for yourself to do what you feel like doing. Meniere's can make you feel that you must give up your goals, hopes and dreams. From my experience, the opposite is true.

Set your expectations like this: "I will go beyond the limits of my Meniere's, I will find a way to do whatever it is I want to do." You can learn a list of new things like I did. You can do all the things you love doing and more. Getting and keeping active should be part of your wellness plan. Even if you can't always do what you planned at the time, keep trying.

Self-esteem increases with successful experiences and by having a sense of purpose. From learning new things, getting active, and going out as much as you can to enjoy yourself, comes the heady gratification that you are living your life despite having Meniere's disease. The more you can do, the better you feel.

Move away from the emotional inertia disease can cause. Define what you want and then make it happen. You can travel in a plane, go on holiday, and climb to the top of the Eiffel Tower in Paris, if that is what you want to do. You just won't be able to fly a commercial aircraft or scuba dive. But then you can snorkel. You are virtually unlimited.

To achieve your goals you just need to do a couple of things: **Conserve energy. Ask for help when you need it.**

Use your talents! Find ways to ways to boost your self-esteem into the positive. The more things you can do the better: art, writing, music, gardening, educational classes, playing cards, dancing, biking, hiking, looking after animals.

Nature is a healing force. In our lives we need more than food and drink. For optimum health, we need fresh air, sun, water and the calming effects of nature on our mind and body. Try to include nature in your day. Tune in and focus on nature. The sound of birdsong for example is known to have a calming meditative effect. The sound of crickets or cicadas. The rustle of leaves. Tune in to your sense of smell: the grass, flowers, and the air after it rains. By trying new things or getting back in touch with things you loved doing will give you a much needed inner tranquillity.

Meniere's can help you understand and appreciate your talents and strengths you have. As you get in touch with those things you have always loved doing, you'll find, by coping in this way with Meniere's, you'll develop creatively. Then anything is possible. When you find ways back to "your self" you see Meniere's from another perspective.

It is only when you are challenged and out of your comfort zone, that you find an inner resilience. Personal resilience is your individual internal powers of being emotionally stronger than your physical self. It may be a factor you might not have known.

At times, Meniere's takes you closer to invaluable inner resources. When a customary pattern of living has been shattered by illness, you fear that you are no longer recognizable as a whole being. The belief in your self-worth rarely emerges until what you have lost and grieved for is replaced by precious moments of inner peace and joy. This leads to a reconstruction of the sense of oneself as a cohesive, intact entity. The reconstruction takes on many concrete aspects, such as the development of new skills, but the most important value is emotional. It is the re-emergence of a positive self-image that constitutes reconstruction of your life.

Hope is the most crucial emotion we need. Feeling hopeful gives us a reason to bother trying. How much hope you feel is up to you. You can give yourself none, a little or a lot. Be generous. If hope is a feeling you create by how you think. Then think about positive things in your life, no matter how small.

POSITIVE EFFECTS OF THE PRESENT SIMPLE

Practice living life in the present. Moment by moment. It is easier said than done, because your mind has a habit of getting in the way. You have to practice neither looking too far backward or too far forward. If you are only looking backward, you carry the past over your shoulder.

Focusing on how things were before you were diagnosed with Meniere's does not get you through the Meniere days. If you use all your emotional energy considering how things were before the Meniere's and comparing it to how things are now, it is very self-punishing. If you sense this going on, you need to work at changing this. Moving forward towards better health is the aim.

Physical discomfort increases when you are ill. Your anxiety levels increase as well. Don't let yourself drop down into the black hole of negative thought. Try to stay positive. If you get too down on your situation, you create more internal stress. And the less stress you have the better for your overall well being. So when you find yourself having regular thoughts like "I am never going to get better". Identify the thought and take a look at it. If a thought makes you feel hopeless, get rid of it. If a thought makes you feel worse and not better about you and your situation, then it's time to do some mental house clearing.

You can clear recurring negative thoughts from your mind with one word. The word is stop. When you hear the same recurring thought in your mind. You say "stop" and you quit that thought. Then you replace the negative thought with a positive one. "I will get well". "I am getting better with every breath". When you do this you start to eliminate negative thoughts about your condition.

If you actively find the flip side of the negative, you'll discover the power of positive thinking works. Thinking positively and rationally is a valuable tool to use when you are coping with Meniere's. Your belief system is programmed by you. If you want to regain you life, it won't happen with negative black hole thinking. Control your thoughts and change them and you'll find it easier to manage Meniere's symptoms.

Focus on things that give you hope. Spend time each day thinking about positive things. Work on changing negative focus to a positive one. Mind over body. Take note of the positive; the successes that happens in your day, to you and anyone in your world. Pay attention to the positives. This can only be done if you have already mastered the skill of living fully in the present. You can do this by practicing relaxation techniques, meditation, and your own internal capacity to let those positives resonate inside. Once you master this rather metaphysical element you will find you have a wonderful resource of constant renewable energy.

If you are not looking back at the past or worried about the future you can live in the moment with consciousness, patience, compassion, and appreciation for yourself and others. If you are doing this, you are already much better.

THE NO EFFECT

Saying no is a powerful energy conservation tool. Practice asserting yourself. Learn to say no. Some people find this tiny word too hard to say. No is not an easy word. No does not roll off the tongue. No sounds like a short, hard slap. No is not a gentle word. But it is a powerful word.

You have to learn to say no. Use the word no to protect your energy reserves. Try not to add extra things to make up for saying no. No, you don't need to give explanations. No, you don't need to justify your actions. You can let people know exactly what you want to do and what you don't want to do. Simply say no, if your energy is low. It's up to you to give yourself a break, because no one else will.

THE EFFECT OF PLANNING

When you suffer with Meniere's symptoms, the random nature of vertigo attacks makes your everyday life unpredictable. That's why you need to plan your days. You do this by making a timetable. A daily schedule of activities for yourself. You create a structure. Most everything in life has structure. It is the framework, an outline of what you're planning to do for the day. You can be flexible within that plan. You make every day, your day. If you keep to a daily plan, you can tick off the things you have wanted to do and have managed to do. When you can get things done, even a few things during the week, it's a start.

A personal management plan can be as simple as deciding to walk around the block each morning. It can be as quiet as closing your eyes and meditating. Or as rejuvenating as standing under the shower and letting the water run down your spine. After you set a plan in place, you will be amazed at how much better you feel.

After a few weeks of following your daily schedules, you will be able to look back and see how far you have come to recovering a sense of well-being in your life. And when you start putting measures in place to regain your health, your overall health will improve. The healthier you are, the less severe the symptoms are. That is how I found it.

When you have a plan, you will find that you will do most things you wanted to. You will see that Meniere's does not happen every minute of every day. O.K you will have bad afternoons. Or a bad day. Make a schedule. You'll maintain a sense of forward momentum. Remember small steps.

Better to achieve many small things, than fail at the big things. I call it Zen of the Ant.

AN EFFECTIVE WAY OF MOVING ON

Here is an example of a basic day plan for the early days of Meniere's.

7-7:30 am.
Sit up in bed.
If someone can draw the curtains, open the window and let fresh air in, even better. And bring you a drink. Three teaspoons of lemon or lime with a teaspoon or so of honey in hot water. This picks up your blood sugar levels to kick start your day.

8 am.
Get up slowly. Take a shower. Don't be in a hurry. Let the water run down your back. Shake your hands to clear negative energy

away from your body. Focus on the water as a way to get rid of negative ions with the aim of a new day and a fresh start to it.

8:30 am.
Have breakfast.

9:00 am.
Walk to the local cafe or around the block. The aim is to increase your walking time in small increments. Hydrate.

10 am.
Rest on the sofa. Practice meditation. Drink and eat a small snack.

11 am.
Get with nature. Go for a walk in the garden. Or sit outside. Or stand barefoot on the grass. If you have a pool, get in. If you feel like it, relax with a long soak in the bath. Include a few drops of essential oils for relaxation in the water.

12. noon.
Make and eat a nutritious lunch.

1. pm.
Practice breathing exercises. Rest.

2. pm.
Read. Write in your diary.

2:30 pm.
Go for a walk.

3: 30 pm.
Call a friend for a chat. Stay in touch.

4:00 pm.
Complete something you have started. A letter. A book.

6: 00 pm.
Make dinner.

7: 00 pm.
Go for an early evening walk.

8: 00 pm.
Watch TV or listen to music. Music can relax and promote a sense of wellbeing.

9.30 pm.
Go to bed. Sleep peacefully.

THE DIARY EFFECT

Start to work on recognizing the warning signs of recurring symptoms. Often you can reduce the chance of a full blown vertigo attack, if you act quickly. The book *Vertigo Vertigo'* details triggers and stages of Meniere's attacks to help you recognize the stages and symptoms.

Keep a diary and identify patterns and episodes. Be specific about dates, times of vertigo attacks. Decide what elements in your life: whether food, lack of sleep, crisis in your work, overwork, family, weather, emotional life are likely to have triggered vertigo attacks. Work on trying to eliminate, resolve or change these stresses.

THE STRESS EFFECT

My specialist told me to walk away from stress in my life. He was right. Whenever I let myself go into a stress mode, I would usually have a vertigo attack. Stress created fallout. If I was under any stress then a vertigo attack would happen within the days following. Stress was a major factor in my vertigo attacks. The vertigo attack ratio of stress featured in my dairy entries. Take stress like you do salt. Live with less!

Since stress is a well-known trigger for Meniere's attacks, it is important that you take steps to avoid stress in your life. Ironically, suffering with Meniere's creates the most stress in your life. Stress comes with being ill. Not only do you have a knock on effect from illness, but in everyday life there are other stresses

It is important to recognize the things that cause you stress in your life. When you know exactly what gives you stress, you can figure out ways to cope or avoid that stress. List the stressors in your diary and watch out for them.

Meet your stresses

Physical:

When you put your body under stress; by staying up late, spending too much time on one activity; abusing alcohol or recreational drugs, getting overtired, extremes of temperature, a cold or flu, not eating properly, not drinking enough. These are some examples of physical stressors on your body.

Emotional And Mental Stress:

All the small, serious, unsolvable and complicated things that play on your mind. And replay in your sleep. From worries and anxiety about living conditions, money, children, relationship problems, arguments, moving house, a new job or loss of job, achievement, success, winning money, visitors, illness, holidays, birth of a child, loss of a parent, legal issues, to changes in the workplace. It's these personal dynamics in your life that are likely to trigger a vertigo attack.

So one of the first things you need to do is make a list of things that have stressed you out. Look back over the past six months. The stress from past events can still affect you months later. So look at the past six months and include all the things that happened recently. From the list, you can do some creative thinking or lateral thinking about the ways you can cope with the stress.

THE MENIERE EFFECT ON YOU

Take care of you. Strengthen your healthy habits of getting enough sleep, eating well and stressing less. Give up unhealthy habits.

Make a to do list for the week. Do the important jobs first. Avoid doing things in a rush. Stop being rushed and overly busy. Organize your time to make your days easier by planning ahead. Let unimportant things go.

Avoid overworking. Schedule rests and breaks during the day. Don't let yourself run ragged. Recognize when you feel tired and rest. Don't keep going at a task to finish the job. Notice the minute you start to feel tired or overwhelmed and stop immediately. Take a rest. Stop and drink. Eat nutritious snacks. You can't afford to run on empty.

You may have too much on your plate, so delegate and share responsibilities to free up your time. Say no without feeling guilty.

Practice breathing. Meditate. You may have to ask someone to help you reduce stress. For example: if you feel you don't get enough time to yourself to meditate and practice your breathing, then let your partner know that you need quiet time.

Try to get plenty of sleep. If you have a bad night, catch up on sleep you have missed. Generate pleasure in your life. Plan regular breaks. Make time for activities that you love to do. Have more fun. Laugh more. Keep company with healthy, positive, supportive people.

THE SABOTEUR EFFECT

Check this question: do you sometimes seem to sabotage yourself? Do you sometimes do things that might exasperate your symptoms and cause a vertigo attack? Like work too hard, not get enough sleep, take hold of an argument and don't let go, raise your voice, and order a margarita cocktail with a salt encrusted rim.

When you are determined to order an espresso instead of your usual decaffeinated coffee, something is going on with you! You are obviously feeling better. Well enough to set challenges for yourself. If you are thinking and acting like this, it's a good sign. Instead of downsizing your life, you are doing the opposite. You are pushing at your limits and that's what you should be doing. This is a normal reaction and you're testing your boundaries at this point. Eventually you'll find you can do most of these things without the attacks. You'll find new boundaries that work for you. Then you'll test those ones.

As well as the positive saboteur effect which is a way of testing boundaries, we can use our relationships with other people as a way of measuring our condition. Be careful with this. This could seriously sabotage your relationships at work or at home.

You may deliberately use a misunderstanding to place blame on someone else and have an argument. You stay in the argument to see how far you can take the argument without having a vertigo attack. You may have allowed yourself to do too much, knowing that the likely outcome of too much work is a Meniere's attack. Sometimes you will get away with doing this. But the best plan is to catch yourself before you start to go into this kind of sabotage mode.

THE RELAXATION EFFECT

TRY TO DO THIS TWICE A DAY

To relax you mind…first relax your body.
This relaxation will make you feel calmer.
For a deep sense of total relaxation you need
to work from your feet up to your head.
Relax areas of your body, one by one.

TEN STEP RELAXATION

1.
Choose a quiet place where you won't be
interrupted. Let others know you are taking
time out and close the door. Lie down and
get comfortable. If you can't lie down flat,
put a pillow under your head or sit in a chair.

2.
Close your eyes.

3.

Inhale slowly and deeply. Do this for three breaths.

4.

Relax your mind.

5.

Beginning with your toes on both feet, tense the muscles tightly. Hold for ten seconds. Relax your toes for 15 seconds.

6.

Keep breathing. Inhale and exhale.

7.

Using this tension and relaxing technique. Tense up and relax all your body.

8.

Moving from your toes to your left and right ankles. Tense and relax both at the same time.

9.

Then your calves, knees, thighs, hips, butt, stomach, chest. Fingers, forearms, upper arms, shoulders, neck and back. Your jaw, your eyes (frown and raise your eyebrows).

10.

When you have completed tensing and relaxing all your body parts, then tense your whole body for ten seconds, then relax your body for 30 seconds. Repeat this tensing and relaxing of your whole body three more times.

Notice how calm and relaxed you become. Stay in this state for as long as you feel comfortable.

TWENTY EFFECTIVE WAYS TO MANAGE MENIERE'S

1.
Buy a new diary.

Aim to write in the diary each day.

If you miss a day, catch up. Write down how it is for you.

The diary acts as a map, a self-discovery on the journey of Meniere's.

2.
Set personal goals.

Read as much as you can about Meniere's.

Decide what aspects of your life you need to work on.

Do you need to get more exercise.

Alter your diet. Reduce your salt intake.

Make a list of goals you want to achieve.

When you reach one goal, set another one.

3.
Keep track of changes.

Write down notes about changes you are making.

What positive steps have you taken for your health.

Make healthy decisions.

4.
Write down a vitamin regime.

You can read up on supplements in *Meniere Man Let's Get Better.*

Start with single vitamin supplements.

Try Vitamin E and Vitamin C for starters.

Take extra vitamins to boost your system.

5.
Daily exercise routine.

Just start walking step by step.

Get moving. Keep moving.

Do a little more than you feel like doing.

Aim to walk twice a day.

Make markers. Count lamp posts.

Time your walking sessions.

Increase duration of walks.

Walk in the evening.

Do physical activities you enjoy.

6.
Listen to your body.

Tune in to your body.

Avoid overdoing it.

Take regular breaks.

Have a rest.

Act on body reactions.

Know when your body is under stress.

Stop if you are aware of stress.

7.
Harness the power of nature.

Sun. Sea. Fresh air. Food and water.

Let nature keep your body in balance.

Stand barefoot on grass and feel grounded.

Watch a sunset.

Listen to an early morning bird chorus.

Sit on the seashore.

Lie in the sand.

Breathe the air. Feel more alive.

8.
Water.

Drink mineral water high in magnesium.

Drink water low in sodium.

Avoid carbonated water as the salt content is higher.

Take long showers.

Lie in the bath. Use essential oils to relax.

Swim.

9.
Be your own best friend.

Practice being patient with yourself.

Treat yourself like a friend.

Do more for you.

Take care of yourself.

Allow time out, time off, delegate tasks.

Let others share the load.

Focus on your needs.

Put yourself first.

10.
Stay socially connected.

Spend time with friends.

Phone someone.

Laugh.

Go out.

Have fun.

Small things count big time.

Do what you love to do.

11.
Increase fitness levels.

Do daily exercise.

Walk.

Yoga.

Tai Chi.

Enroll in a gym. Get a program set by a personal trainer.

Train with a friend.

Get a set of stretching exercises.

Do core balance work with a trained instructor.

Be unlimited.

12.
Write out an eating plan.

Try eating 6 small meals a day.

Cook foods you love but change the recipes to reduce salt.

Throw the salt shaker away.

Replace salt with herbs.

Don't bring salted food into the house.

Throw out salted foods from the pantry.

Clear salted foods out of the fridge.

Go shopping for low salt items.

Plant a herb garden.

Keep a food section in your diary.

Stop carbonated drinks, too much sugar.

Do the math and check what your average daily intake of sodium is.

Ask your doctor to refer you to a nutritionist or dietician.

13.
Look at alternative therapies.

Acupuncture.

Massage.

Cranial manipulation.

Homeopathy.

Aroma therapy.

Biofeedback.

14.
Find Inner Peace.

Meditate twice a day.

Do a guided meditation.

Make up a personal healing mantra.

Write affirmations down.

Get meditation CDs.

15.
Do regular personal reviews.

What's working for you?

How are you feeling?

What do you want to change?

16.
Personal challenges.

What are your main triggers?

What are your main stresses?

What adjustments do you have to make?

Have you laughed lately?

Subscribe to the comedy channel.

Love a lot.

Relax.

17.
Small steps count to wellness.

Book in a massage.

Go swimming.

Have a picnic.

Get out more.

Paint.

Write.

Learn a musical instrument.

Do sport.

Get a pet.

18.
Focus on what life means for you.

It's a personal choice. You get the idea. It is about giving yourself what you need. Looking after yourself. Making each day count. It is about living. Even with this disease. Make everything a step forward.

Not every moment is a Meniere's moment.

19.
Believe in your ability to get better.

20.
Spread your wings. Fly as far as you can.

EFFECTIVE MENIERE'S SUPPORT NETWORKS AND SOCIETIES

Meniere's Society (UNITED KINGDOM)
www. menieres.org.uk
Meniere's Society Australia (AUSTRALIA)
info@menieres.org.au
The Meniere's Resource & Information Centre (AUSTRALIA) www.menieres.org.au
Healthy Hearing & Balance Care (AUSTRALIA)
www.healthyhearing.com.au
Vestibular Disorders association (AUSTRALIA)
www.vestibular .org
The Dizziness and Balance Disorders Centre (AUSTRALIA) www.dizzinessbalancedisorders.com
Meniere's Research Fund Inc (AUSTRALIA)

www.menieresresearch.org.au
Australian Psychological Society APS (AUSTRALIA)
www.psychology.org.au
Meniere's Disease Information Center (USA)
www.menieresinfo.com

Vestibular Disorders Association (USA)
www.vestibular.org
BC Balance and Dizziness Disorders Society (CANADA) www.balanceand dizziness.org
Hearwell (NEW ZEALAND)
www.hearwell.co.nz
WebMD. www.webmd.com
National Institute for Health
www.medlineplus.gov
Mindful Living Program
www.mindfullivingprograms.com
Center for Mindfulness
www. umassmed.edu.com

ABOUT MENIERE MAN

This bestselling author is an Australian born writer with a background as an award-winning Creative Director, Executive Director and partner in a successful advertising agency. Today he is an author of twelve books including four Bestsellers and two #1 Bestsellers.

At the height of his business career and aged just forty-six, he suddenly became acutely ill. He was diagnosed with Meniere's disease. He began to loose all hope that he would fully recover his health. However the full impact of having Meniere's disease was to come later. He lost not only his health, but his career and financial status as well.

It was his personal spirit and desire to get "back to normal" that turned his life around for the better. He decided that you can't put a limit on anything in life. Rather than letting Meniere's disease get in the way of life, he started to focus on what to do about overcoming Meniere's disease.

With the advice on healing and recovery in his books, anyone reading the advice given, can make simple changes and find a way toward a recovery from Meniere's disease.

These days life is different for the Author. He is a fit older man who has no symptoms of Meniere's except for tinnitus and hearing loss in one ear. He does not take any medication. All the physical activities he enjoys these days require a high degree of balance: snowboarding, surfing, hiking, windsurfing, weightlifting, and riding a motorbike. All these things he started to do while suffering with Meniere's disease symptoms.

Meniere Man believes that if you want to experience a marked improvement in health you can't wait until you feel well to start. You must begin to improve your health, even though you don't feel like it.

With a smile and a sense of humor, the Author pens himself as Meniere Man, because, as he says, Meniere's disease changed his life dramatically. Today the Author is a writer, painter, designer and exhibiting artist. He is married to a writer. They have two adult children. He spends his time writing and painting. He loves the sea, cooking, travel, photography, nature and the company of family, friends and his beloved dog.

ADDITIONAL INFORMATION

If you enjoyed this book and you think it could be helpful to others, please leave a review for the book at amazon.com. amazon.co.uk or Goodreads. Thank you.

This book and other Meniere Man books are available worldwide from international booksellers and local bookstores including Amazon.com, Amazon.co.uk, Barnes & Noble Books. Available in paperback and Kindle.

MENIERE MAN BOOKS

Let's Get Better
A Memoir of Meniere's Disease
#1 BEST SELLER

Let's Get Better CD
Relaxing & Healing Guided Meditation

**Meniere Man And The Film Director.
The Self Help Book For Meniere's
VERTIGO**

Vertigo Vertigo
About Vertigo About Dizziness and What You Can Do About it.

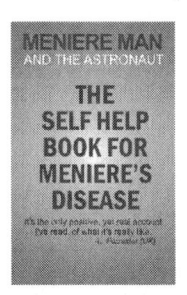

Meniere Man And The Astronaut
The Self Help Book for Meniere's Disease
#1 BEST SELLER

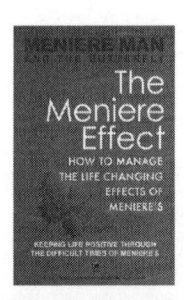

**Meniere Man And The Butterfly
The Meniere Effect**
How to Manage The Life Changing Effects Of Meniere's

Meniere Man In The Kitchen. Recipes That Helped Me Get Over Meniere's
Delicious nutritious low salt recipes from our family kitchen.
#1 BEST SELLER

Meniere Man In The Kitchen. BOOK 2. Recipes That Helped Me Get Over Meniere's

#1 BEST SELLER

Meniere Man In The Himalayas. Cooking Low Salt Curries In The Kitchens Of India

Meniere Man In The Kitchen. Cooking For Meniere's The Low Salt Way. ITALIAN.

Printed in Great Britain
by Amazon